Acknowledgements

Nne Rose Nnennaya
Nne nne Nwanyimma, Ufoaku, Virginia,
Amaraegbulem
Nna Paul Mbadiwe
Nna nna Ohaeri, Gabriel Amuchie
Sister Bev
Brother Ik and Uzoma
Sisters Ofunne, Ijeoma, Femi, Laura, Pam, Rolake
All of my mothers
All of my grandmothers
All of my sisters
Both living and floating

D1616853

NO LONGER PROPERTY OF
ANYTHINK LIBRARIES/
RANGEVIEW LIBRARY DISTRICT

"I write to do away with the lies I tell myself
The lies society tells me
The lies I once believed
I have to keep writing them away
I have to stop believe in them
I have to start believing in myself
I have to keep writing."
- Nnennaya Amuchie

I. Birth

Almost every Nigerian woman
Has miscarried
Didn't you know?
Giving birth can be a death sentence
Your life or theirs
Sometimes both

How many of your grandmothers died trying to
carry your life into existence?

Have you asked?
You demand child birth
You ask her to keep it
You ask her to reproduce for you
As if you are a nine-month long morphine pill

Luckily my mothers survived

My mother's name is
Nnennaya
And out of my mother's womb, here I was
Nnennaya
Nne, mother
Nna, father
Ya, mine
My father's mother, grandmother
My grandfather's mother, great-grandmother
Apparently we have a lot of unfinished
business to handle

He gleefully walks into the house at 5 a.m.
Still expecting his breakfast before he showers
for work
Filled with no shame
She begins to open her mouth to speak
She hesitates and decides against it
She no longer has the strength

She repeats to herself
You must stay and endure
You must stay and endure
You must stay and endure
He is your husband
And you are his wife

Mothers shrink themselves
To the men in their lives
Creating a bridge for their children
To crossover this life
Into a freely newly liberated world
Where black girl joy reigns
But our mothers are scared and scarred
Overprotective knowing the battles they
had to fight crawling over their mothers
bruised backs
She once slipped into
the cracks of grandmother's spine
Getting caught up in that same toxic love
I hope I never
But I know I may have to
One day

I learned to hate my mother and love my father.
Constant battle between the two.
Always getting dragged into their shit.
Dad said mom was crazy because
all she did was yell and yell and yell.
But mom said she didn't yell.
She said she was raising her voice.
Because after suffering in silence,
her voice was the most powerful thing she had.
But I didn't get it then.
All I saw her do was yell and yell and yell.

Terrible husbands
Wonderful fathers
The men in our lives who show us how
to fight and persevere are the same ones
who fought the woman out of our mothers
and so we are stuck
Living while our mothers are dying
for the love and attention he gave to
Daddy's little girl

Resentful mothers find themselves
Encouraging their daughters to
Marry
Settle
Have children and be good wives
All the things that made them question
Their worth
Value
And place on this earth
Near death praying to God asking
for another chance at life
And so there's a daughter
Inches away from falling into the
trap created by her mother's words

In a culture of silence
Let the pen be your weapon
The ink is permanent and can transcend
emotions and stories across mediums
into the future
Weaponize your pen and destroy
The culture of silence

My name is Nnennaya
And my grandmothers came to me in my sleep
And whispered
You have unfinished business

Get to work

Get to work Get to work Get to work Get to work Get to work
Get to work Get to work Get to work Get to work
Get to work Get to work Get to work
Get to work Get to work
Get to work
Get to work Get to work Get to work Get to work Get to work
Get to work Get to work Get to work Get to work
Get to work Get to work Get to work
Get to work Get to work
Get to work
Get to work
Get to work Get to work
Get to work Get to work Get to work
Get to work Get to work Get to work Get to work
Get to work Get to work Get to work Get to work Get to work
Get to work Get to work Get to work Get to work Get to work
Get to work Get to work Get to work Get to work
Get to work Get to work Get to work
Get to work Get to work
Get to work
Get to work Get to work Get to work Get to work Get to work
Get to work Get to work Get to work Get to work
Get to work Get to work Get to work
Get to work Get to work
Get to work
Get to work Get to work Get to work Get to work Get to work
Get to work Get to work Get to work Get to work
Get to work Get to work Get to work
Get to work Get to work
Get to work
Get to work
Get to work Get to work
Get to work Get to work Get to work
Get to work Get to work Get to work Get to work
Get to work Get to work Get to work Get to work Get to work
Get to work Get to work Get to work Get to work Get to work
Get to work Get to work Get to work Get to work
Get to work Get to work Get to work
Get to work Get to work
Get to work

II. Anger

I

angry angry angry angry angry angry angry angry angry angry angry angry angry
angry angry angry angry angry angry angry angry angry angry angry angry angry
angry angry angry angry angry angry angry angry angry angry angry angry angry

AM

angry angry angry angry angry angry angry angry angry angry angry angry angry
angry angry angry angry angry angry angry angry angry angry angry angry angry
angry angry angry angry angry angry angry angry angry angry angry angry angry

FUCKING

angry angry angry angry angry angry angry angry angry angry angry angry angry
angry angry angry angry angry angry angry angry angry angry angry angry angry
angry angry angry angry angry angry angry angry angry angry angry angry angry

ANGRY

angry angry angry angry angry angry angry angry angry angry angry angry angry
angry angry angry angry angry angry angry angry angry angry angry angry angry
angry angry angry angry angry angry angry angry angry angry angry angry angry

I

angry angry angry angry angry angry angry angry angry angry angry angry angry
angry angry angry angry angry angry angry angry angry angry angry angry angry
angry angry angry angry angry angry angry angry angry angry angry angry angry

AM

angry angry angry angry angry angry angry angry angry angry angry angry angry
angry angry angry angry angry angry angry angry angry angry angry angry angry
angry angry angry angry angry angry angry angry angry angry angry angry angry

ANGRY

angry angry angry angry angry angry angry angry angry angry angry angry angry
angry angry angry angry angry angry angry angry angry angry angry angry angry
angry angry angry angry angry angry angry angry angry angry angry angry angry

AS

angry angry angry angry angry angry angry angry angry angry angry angry angry
angry angry angry angry angry angry angry angry angry angry angry angry angry
angry angry angry angry angry angry angry angry angry angry angry angry angry

FUCK
EXCUSE MY ENGLISH

Sitting at the edge of my bed
Waiting to take it all away
All of the pain
All of my sorrow
I have consumed too many tears
and all I have left is anger
I am entitled to my anger because I am angry
Because I am angry
Because I am angry
My explanation for being angry is
Because
I
am
angry
And nothing and no one can change that

My anger fuels me
It gives me hope
This anger lets me know I am still alive
Alive after many nights at the edge of my bed
Waiting to take it all away
Waiting to give up on this world
I never wanted to be immortal

Until I experienced the burning sensation
Of anger all throughout my veins
I know you don't think a black woman
like me should love her anger
Plant her anger
Water her anger
Grow her anger
But every day I keep getting angrier
I'd rather be angry than sad

I bet you want this black woman
to be sad all the time
I bet you want her to mope around everywhere

Everyday
Every damn day

You want me to be the victim so
you can control my emotions!!!!!!!!!!!
You want to control me

doncha'?

But you cannot control an angry black woman
You cannot control me
I am angry and I am in a constant state of rage
You do not frighten me
You cannot control me
You do not own me, my mind, or my body

Are you scared yet?
Are you scared of the angry black woman?
Who doesn't give a motherfucking shit about
what the fuck you have to fucking say about
a nigga like her

That escalated quickly
Do I still scare you? Be weary afraid.
I will wear you out until you
recognize the power in my anger.
I will make you wish you never ___ _____ _____

Fill in the blanks.

II½. Angrier

I am grateful. Because without this anger, I could not go on. My anger is valid and necessary. My anger compels me to relate, build, and rejoice with my black sisters. My anger made me love myself unapologetically and go where I am loved always. My anger led to me to say no when I wanted to and yes when I needed to. My anger guides me in ways that my sadness and joy cannot. My anger is grounded in love for black women because how can such amazing human beings be hated so much and treated so poorly. How could these women be so resilient with the little scraps of the world? Making lemonade out of lemons?

Huh. Bey?

Black girls are magic because we have been pushed to create magic. When you find someone just as angry as you are in the world, you begin to create fire. Black girl juju. Eerie but powerful. Fascinating yet frightening. Black girls are creating fires that everyone wants to see put out. But we are deserted and dehydrated, so more and more girls are catching on fire. Mmiri no dey for here oooooo.

We are burning incense and roots and oils for our ancestors who speak through us, in us, for us. We are angry for our mothers, grandmothers, great grandmothers, and all the women who made fire between their palms. For all the women who found fire between their thighs and through the wave of their tongues. Their legacy will never die down as long as my anger is grounded in love. As long as I remember that love and anger are not opposites. As long as I am able to articulate and re-define my anger for myself, my anger will always be necessary. And even when I don't have the words, my actions or inaction will guide me.

I will go where I am loved, always.
I will always remember the complexities of my humanity. I will always remember that while the love is minimal, it is ever-burning.

Fire emits light and heat and so our love and anger will emit light and heat. The light at the end of the journey is that black girls everywhere will one day know and embody freedom while the warmth and heat of love and sisterhood will reinforce and affirm this freedom.

My anger will free me, one day. Our anger will free us, some day. And all we will have left is combustion of love. We will have the fuel to come together, the oxygen to breathe life in one another, and the energy to sustain one another.

Freedom

Freedom Freedom Freedom Freedom Freedom Freedom Freedom
Freedom Freedom Freedom Freedom Freedom Freedom Freedom
Freedom Freedom Freedom Freedom Freedom Freedom Freedom
Freedom Freedom Freedom Freedom Freedom Freedom Freedom
Freedom Freedom Freedom Freedom Freedom Freedom Freedom
Freedom Freedom Freedom Freedom Freedom Freedom Freedom
Freedom Freedom Freedom Freedom Freedom Freedom Freedom
Freedom Freedom Freedom Freedom Freedom Freedom Freedom
Freedom Freedom Freedom Freedom Freedom Freedom Freedom
Freedom Freedom Freedom Freedom Freedom Freedom Freedom
Freedom Freedom Freedom Freedom Freedom Freedom Freedom
Freedom Freedom Freedom Freedom Freedom Freedom Freedom
Freedom Freedom Freedom Freedom Freedom Freedom Freedom
Freedom Freedom Freedom Freedom Freedom Freedom Freedom
Freedom Freedom Freedom Freedom Freedom Freedom Freedom

What is freedom?

Freedom Freedom Freedom Freedom Freedom Freedom Freedom
Freedom Freedom Freedom Freedom Freedom Freedom Freedom
Freedom Freedom Freedom Freedom Freedom Freedom Freedom
Freedom Freedom Freedom Freedom Freedom Freedom Freedom
Freedom Freedom Freedom Freedom Freedom Freedom Freedom
Freedom Freedom Freedom Freedom Freedom Freedom Freedom
Freedom Freedom Freedom Freedom Freedom Freedom Freedom
Freedom Freedom Freedom Freedom Freedom Freedom Freedom
Freedom Freedom Freedom Freedom Freedom Freedom Freedom
Freedom Freedom Freedom Freedom Freedom Freedom Freedom
Freedom Freedom Freedom Freedom Freedom Freedom Freedom
Freedom Freedom Freedom Freedom Freedom Freedom Freedom
Freedom Freedom Freedom Freedom Freedom Freedom Freedom

Do you know what freedom is?

Freedom Freedom Freedom Freedom Freedom Freedom Freedom
Freedom Freedom Freedom Freedom Freedom Freedom Freedom
Freedom Freedom Freedom Freedom Freedom Freedom Freedom
Freedom Freedom Freedom Freedom Freedom Freedom Freedom
Freedom Freedom Freedom Freedom Freedom Freedom Freedom
Freedom Freedom Freedom Freedom Freedom Freedom Freedom
Freedom Freedom Freedom Freedom Freedom Freedom Freedom
Freedom Freedom Freedom Freedom Freedom Freedom Freedom
Freedom Freedom Freedom Freedom Freedom Freedom Freedom
Freedom Freedom Freedom Freedom Freedom Freedom Freedom
Freedom Freedom Freedom Freedom Freedom Freedom Freedom
Freedom Freedom Freedom Freedom Freedom Freedom Freedom
Freedom Freedom Freedom Freedom Freedom Freedom Freedom
Freedom Freedom Freedom Freedom Freedom Freedom Freedom
Freedom Freedom Freedom Freedom Freedom Freedom Freedom
Freedom Freedom Freedom Freedom Freedom Freedom Freedom
Freedom Freedom Freedom Freedom Freedom Freedom Freedom
Freedom Freedom Freedom Freedom Freedom Freedom Freedom
Freedom Freedom Freedom Freedom Freedom Freedom Freedom

III. Desire

My mother never talked to me about fucking, so I had
to learn it all by myself.

At first
I closed my legs
Preserving myself for him
Because that's what *good girls* do
Finally, the day came
And boy was I disappointed
The disappointing wait
A fire burning between my legs is what happens
when two dry things rub together causing friction
neither one of us knew what we were doing
Even though he said he'd been here before
But that's what they all say
I thought, how many other lies had I been told?
What would it take for a girl to cum?
                !Mississippi Goddamn!

But soon, it got better. Well, a little better. I thought
sex would free me from the chains of my ancestors,
finally liberated and finally in control of my body.

And so
I fucked him for all of the nights
My grandmother had to sleep alone
Knowing her husband had two other wives
And maybe a few more mistresses
And probably some distant children
The lonely nights
The dry harmattan nights
A gust of wind hits her chest
nne nne awakes from a sneeze
Turns around and realizes
That feeling of warmth was but a dream
Fifteen years of age

Married into patriarchy
_{Fuck patriarchy} **Fuck patriarchy** **Fuck patriarchy**
Decades of pleasure ripped away
So I take a deep breath and order him
Enter
↑ Cum this ↗ way →

I was more in charge of my body. More aware.
More alive. More me. More I.
I dictated my pleasure every single time.

And I fucked for Nigerian girls, *dem*

For Nigerian girls who have never felt the
deep vibrations stemming from the clitoris
They are taught is dirty
For the Nigerian girls whose pleasure
was ripped by the tip of a sharp knife because
It is our culture; don't you know?
Women who seek pleasure are evil!
They are dirty, ignoramus whores
Look at this ashawo![i]
Look at me, the ashawo!

The body they are taught is bad
Unholy
Undeserving
Lacking of pleasure
Because of intergenerational guilt
Because of a culture that denies
her the ownership of her pleasure
The ownership of her body and her desires
For the shame
The sleepless nights
thoughts of intimacy fuel her brain
alas she reaches down
1..2 ...3.

\\\\ Stroke ////

And everyone around me knew my mantra
He who does me well
Shall have his brains blown out
Draped in my pearls
Diving deep into my ocean
Well-watered
He sprouts
His hands flow deep inside my tresses
Massaging my temples
As my head rocks up and down
I unleash
He is my Relief
And I ain't talking about Saturday morning at the
salon under the sink, getting my hair rinsed and my
scalp scrubbed
THIS WAS MUCH BETTER

I ask him
All this poetry we are making
Will it ever stop?
Will you ever stop giving me these stanzas?
I feel like I've been here four times before
Coming over and over again (x 2)
Or is it this haiku?
It's like the perfect strokes of paint
At the precise point and don't you dare move
Or I'll kill you, seriously (hehe)
Because I could write poems all day
Narrating this story
All the different characters we play
All the women in me I never knew
I could write them in a free verse,
all the ways you liberate me.
No rules.
No guidelines

I was so twisted at that last climactic ending
Will you ever stop?
Let me know so I can rearrange my schedule

Here I am again. I didn't plan for this but…
Sometimes I would find myself back
between her legs.
Udara[ii]
Tart yet sweet
Stuck in between my lips
I guess you got a little excited
Your favorite fruit
Love,
Udala

Nigerian women who love Nigerian women.
There are many of us.
So get used to it.
Are you reading this with a frown?
Ah-ah! Rejoice and be happy!
Nigerian women loving women will never die,
but the days of me keeping my mouth shut will.

At times, I like being alone and performing
my necessary rituals.
Speaking my many selves back into existence.
One by one.
Reviving all the bodies I buried in him.

Am I Dead or alive?

Uchennaya
Nnennaya
Urennaya
Unu^{iii},
Undress and pull up a 2.99 Walmart vertical mirror
Sit and open your ukwu^{iv}
Do you see that little thing sticking out?
Or maybe yours is bigger than mine
Look at it
What do you see?
Okay, now
Take your finger
Rub it
That shit feels good don't it?
Igbo girls get off too.
No wahala^{v}. The pleasure is (ours).
Self-love

I am alive *again*.
Nnennaya
Grandma, kedu?
O di mma.
Nwam, gawa!
Keep going .

IV. Discovery

As I climaxed, a voice fell down my spine
and into the depths of my soul, invigorating me
It said
You must not carry her burden
You must not carry her pain
You are not your mother's pain
She is not your burden
Someone must break the cycle of chains
Generations of abuse
Someone must finally choose to live for herself.
Let it go.
Let it out.
Girl… Let IT go.
Break the chains.

And it was that day,
I realized I would be okay
No one told me this day would come
The day I
A black girl
Would begin to love myself
I would begin to write myself back into existence
Word by word.
Line by line.
Erasing the generational trauma of my grandmothers
and healing.

And the voice came back up my spine
and out of my mouth
What does happiness look like to you?
Does she gaze at you through the mirror?
even when you have drool hanging from
your ginormous beautiful bottom lip?
and sleep in the creases of your eyes?

When you jump, does she build a
barrier of safety for your perfect landing?

Does she smile? Does she laugh?
Does she allow her body to move to
the rhythm of the world's truth?
Does she feel you?
Na really, does she *feeeel* you?

Does she follow her passions?
Does she embrace your
multidimensional lifestyle?

Does she understand that human beings
like you have layers that are
sometimes not meant to be explored?
Is she taking notes?

Does she give you privacy?
Does she let you cry on her bosom?
Does she rub on your nyash[vi], consensually?
Who is happiness?
Where does she live and
how do you find her?

Does she ever come looking for you?
Is she you?
Are you her?
Figure it out, and keep reading.

V. Rebirth

Over and over again, my sisters save me
In sickness
In good health
In distress
In turmoil
In confusion
In despair
Over and over again, my sisters save me
Black girls save me

I learned to go where you are loved, always
Cherished, always
Supported, always
Respected, always
Genuineness comes from those
who understand, respect, and love you
Those who take you for who you are,
meet you where you're at and encourage you
to **BE** you, always
Easy it is to fall into the cracks of negative
reinforcements and gatekeepers of tough love
A love that is tough can never be tender
Go where you are loved, always
Encouraged, always

How did I end up?
With her?
Damn I'm so amazing
Finding new things to love about myself daily
I used to think there were limits to the depths
I could come to understand myself and
the new ways I could find love in myself
But every day I am shocked
Stunned at the revelations I give to myself
The fondness I grow for myself
I love me so much
Thank you, self.

You make me better, Nnennaya.

Here I am
Facing the world
With a better me
A me that is unapologetically in love with herself
My confidence is unashamed
My guilt is dying
I thought about burying my shame
but I did not want it to come haunt me in my sleep
So I burnt it
The ashes started to rise but quickly
fell down straight into hell
Funny how that works.. gravity

When you end up facing your buried secrets
When you start telling yourself the truth
When you stop running away from
your mother's ghosts
When you start seeking out the
spirits of your grandmother
This is what happens
Don't you see?
You break the chains wrapped around your bones
You begin to speak and feel

You are human
Grandmother said you would have
unfinished business, Anyi emechabele

Gawa[vii]

[i] Igbo word for "whore". I, however, do not believe in the concept of "whore", "hoe", "slut", or any similar terms.

[ii] Nigerian fruit

[iii] Igbo word for "you all/people"

[iv] Igbo word for "legs"

[v] Nigerian Pidgin English word for "no trouble/problem"

[vi] Nigerian Pidgin English word for "buttocks"

[viivii] Igbo word for "Go"

I hope you found yourself in this book.
I hope you answer the next time your ancestors come knocking at your door.
I hope you find love in yourself.
I hope you fall in love with yourself every morning and every night.
A huru m gi nanya.
You are enough.

Ako Na Uche

Professor Udobata R. Onunwa perfectly describes the phrase "Ako Na Uche":

"This is the spiritual force that controls the seat of thoughtfulness, common sense, knowledge, memory and conscience in human beings. People believe that intelligent and resourceful people are endowed with powerful *Ako na uche*, which enables them to face life realities with fortitude, determination, courage, wisdom, and patience. Simple and foolish people are believed to have no or little *Ako na uche*.

Literally, the term is a combination of two words Ako and Uche. While Ako implies tact, skill, and care, Uche means thought and memory. So Ako-na-Uche combines all the human intellects and will power to move on and succeed in life endeavor. It is the difference in the level of human endowment of Ako na Uche that determines human I.Q. in Igbo concept of life.

A person can build up or develop their Ako-na-Uche through understanding wise people, elders, and intelligent persons. In a society that respects age and wisdom, the Igbo accords much honour to old age, which they associate with prudence, patience, wisdom, and reasonableness. When one's conscience pricks them, it is usually believed that their *Ako-na-Uche na ama ya ikpe* – literally implying that one's conscience is judging them – one's conscience is pricking them."

I am guided by all of the women inside of me and all the women before me. The revolutionary Aba women of 1929. I am the Igbo woman's conscience. **Ako na Uche. Daalu. Thank you.**

About the Author

Nnennaya Amuchie is an unapologetic Black Nigerian feminist and writer, unbossed social justice attorney fighting for the day reproductive justice is actualized, prisons and police are abolished, and all black people are free. She was born to two Nigerian immigrants in the city of Angels. A graduate of Santa Clara University (JD/MBA) and the University of California, Davis (B.A.).

Nnennaya has previously published "The Forgotten Victims" How Racialized Gender Stereotypes Lead to Police Violence Against Black Women and Girls: Incorporating an Analysis of Police Violence Into Feminist Jurisprudence and Community Activism" in the Seattle Journal for Social Justice.

She draws inspiration from Igbo culture, her ancestors, and all of the Black people in the diaspora fighting for liberation. Nnennaya believes that we are the ones we have been waiting for and all it takes is one pen to a piece of paper.

@theafrolegalise   Theafrolegalise.com

CPSIA information can be obtained
at www.ICGtesting.com
Printed in the USA
LVOW13s1450170317

527610LV00010B/923/P